Environmental Cybersecurity

Protecting Data and Systems in Climate Change Research

Table of Contents

Chapter 1. Introduction

In this era of rapidly changing climate and related environmental concerns, the need for accurate data and secure systems has never been more critical. Our Special Report takes a comprehensive and accessible look at the often-overlooked, yet pivotal arena of Environmental Cybersecurity: Protecting Data and Systems in Climate Change Research. This report is not heavily technical but drawn from complex concepts, compiled and simplified for your understanding and engagement. Engage with us as we shed light on how experts are tackling environmental data security, the cyber challenges they are facing, and the robust solutions being designed to safeguard the crucial systems driving climate change research. It's an enriching, insightful, and indubitably timely report that will inspire you to be part of the conversation in this indispensable field. Your purchase is a worthwhile investment that contributes to enlightening the world about an essential piece of our planet's future.

Chapter 2. Environmental Cybersecurity: Setting the Scene

The field of environmental cybersecurity has rapidly evolved, borne out of the realization that our climate change data and research systems, too, are susceptible to the wide-ranging impacts of online threats.

Just as global interconnectivity has facilitated leaps in climate change research, it has opened up our vital systems to the potential for cyber vandalism, data breaches, intellectual property theft, and data manipulation. Thus, safeguarding these systems while setting the scene for environmental cybersecurity is a paramount necessity.

2.1. Climate Change and Its Data Transmission

In the world of climate research, vast amounts of intricate data are collected from various sources: from satellites monitoring greenhouse gas emissions to sea buoys checking ocean acidity levels. Highly specialized, synchronized devices generate data that are ingested, processed, analyzed, and archived in data centers often located in different parts of the world.

This real-time data transmission and collaborative sharing among scientists worldwide is undoubtedly invaluable to the understanding and mitigation of climate change. This data abundance, however, invariably increases the susceptibility to cyber-behavior intending to distort or exploit this sensitive information.

2.2. Examples of Environmental Cybersecurity Breaches

To aptly understand the magnitude of the environmental cybersecurity landscape, let's consider some instances in recent history. In 2009, hackers targeted the Climate Research Unit at the University of East Anglia, leading to the release of sensitive emails dubbed 'ClimateGate'. This attack aimed not only to undermine the scientific consensus on human-induced climate change but also to disrupt ongoing international negotiations on climate change regulations.

In another instance, in 2011, over 200 email accounts at the University Corporation for Atmospheric Research came under a phishing attack. By gaining unauthorized access to these accounts, the attackers aimed to gather sensitive data and disrupt weather and climate research.

These incidents underline the fact that protecting environmental data is not merely about securing intellectual property but also pivotal in supporting evidence-based policymaking in our global fight against climate change.

2.3. Challenges to Environmental Cybersecurity

Climate change research is inevitably fraught with multiple challenges. Identifying these issues forms the bedrock of preparing an effective response. The challenges range from technical to the geopolitical arena, and include:

- Data complexity and volume: The sheer physical size of climate datasets, coupled with their intricate complexity, presents significant challenges. Ensuring the secure transmission, accurate interpretation, and storage of these data points is an enormous task.

- Multi-institutional collaboration: Global contribution and shared effort are pillars of climate change research. However, it inevitably promotes a multitude of vulnerabilities, given the varying levels of cybersecurity maturity among institutions.

- The geopolitical aspect: Some countries may be tempted to manipulate climate data to dodge environmental regulations or engage in economic espionage.

- Human error: Sometimes, the weakest link can be unintentional, such as employees inadvertently clicking on malware links or failing to update security patches.

2.4. Building a Robust Cybersecurity Framework

Addressing environmental cybersecurity is not merely a technology problem but a human and institutional challenge as well. Therefore, this would require building a holistic cybersecurity framework.

The first step towards building a robust cybersecurity framework is risk assessment. Every organization involved in climate research needs to understand its unique risks better.

Secondly, the right technology tools need to be in place. These include intrusion detection systems, secure configurations, access control mechanisms, and information protection procedures.

Instilling a culture of cybersecurity throughout the organization is equally important. Strong policies and regular training can significantly increase data security.

Lastly, collaborations must be governed by well-articulated and universally applied cybersecurity standards. Multi-institutional efforts should focus on creating a comprehensive and normative cybersecurity code for the climate research community.

2.5. The Road Ahead

Setting the scene for environmental cybersecurity will necessitate a concerted global response. It requires cultivating a deep understanding of climate data's vulnerabilities and preserving the integrity of climate change research by ensuring data security.

The root challenge in creating effective environmental cybersecurity lies in its inherently collaborative nature. It's clear that it's not a feat to be achieved by individual organizations working in isolation, but rather a task for the global community. Strict cybersecurity guidelines, unifying legislation, improved management of cyber threats, and international cooperation will be essential aspects of this process.

In conclusion, the foundation of effective environmental cybersecurity straddles several aspects, from understanding the challenges to implementing stringent global standards. As we continue to turn to digital methods to understand and combat climate change more effectively, our ability to protect and secure these systems becomes increasingly crucial, shaping the future of our planet.

Chapter 3. Technological Advances in Climate Change Research

Climate change research has come a long way in the last few decades. Aided by breakthroughs in technology, scientists can model, predict, track, and analyze the environmental impacts of global warming with ever-increasing precision. Whether it is collecting data from remote parts of the world or sifting through terabytes of historical weather patterns, technology has undeniably transformed the way we approach climate change.

3.1. Advanced Data Collection Tools

Data collection has always been an integral part of climate change research, and continued advances in technology have made it more effective and efficient. For instance, the use of satellite imagery and remote sensing has become widespread, enabling researchers to track climate phenomena on a global scale. These tools let scientists observe changes in polar ice caps, track sea-level rise, and measure global temperatures from space.

Modern satellites, armed with high-resolution cameras and sensors, can capture minute details of our ecosystems. Such advanced technologies enable continuous monitoring, leading to a comprehensive view of our changing environment. Notably, the use of Lidar (Light Detection and Ranging) technology allows for precise topographic measurements, crucial in flood modeling and forest carbon inventory studies.

Moreover, autonomous devices, including drones and underwater vehicles, provide valuable information on hard-to-reach areas such as deep oceans and dense forests. These autonomous systems can carry various sensors to measure parameters like temperature, humidity, wind speed, and atmospheric pressure. This wealth of data helps construct detailed climate models and forecasts.

3.2. Climate Modeling and Predictive Analytics

Data collection is just the start. Making sense of the vast quantities of information collected is what gives it value. Remarkable strides in climate modeling and predictive analytics have turned enormous datasets into actionable insights.

Advanced modeling tools can create sophisticated simulations, providing detailed projections of how the climate could change in the future. These models take into account a wide array of variables, from ocean current patterns to greenhouse gas emissions, painting an elaborate picture of our planet's climate system.

Predictive analytics, underpinned by machine learning and data mining techniques, have enabled researchers to sift through vast datasets and identify patterns. For instance, these complex algorithms can predict the future spread of wildfires, transition of weather patterns, and the impacts of these on flora and fauna, thus aiding mitigation efforts.

3.3. High Performance Computing

The robust computational power required to handle and analyze vast amounts of data cannot be underestimated. High Performance Computing (HPC) has played a vital role in climate research by providing the ability to process vast datasets and complex simulations rapidly.

Supercomputers, with their ability to perform quadrillions of calculations per second, have been instrumental in developing and refining climate models. These machines take into account numerous variables like wind speed, ocean currents, atmospheric pressure, and greenhouse gas levels to create detailed climate simulations.

Simultaneously, HPC has enabled the use of advanced data analysis methods, such as machine learning algorithms, on large climate datasets. This capability has provided an unprecedented level of insight into the complex mechanisms of climate change.

3.4. Cloud Computing

Cloud computing represents a significant technological advance in climate change research. It allows for the efficient storage and processing of vast amounts of data, enabling researchers from all over the world to collaborate effectively.

Using cloud resources, organizations can store massive data volumes affordably, effectively eliminating the need for physical servers and the associated maintenance costs. Additionally, cloud platforms provide powerful computational power, enabling sophisticated data processing and analysis tasks.

The collaborative possibilities of cloud platforms are also significant. Researchers worldwide can easily access and share data, facilitating interdisciplinary studies and fostering a greater understanding of global climate change impacts.

3.5. Big Data and Machine Learning

The advent of Big Data has profoundly impacted many fields, and climate research is no exception. Big data platforms can manage datasets far larger than traditional databases can handle, enabling comprehensive climate studies.

Machine learning, a subset of artificial intelligence, has also become increasingly valuable in climate research. These algorithms can continually learn from data, improve upon training, and make highly accurate predictions. Whether forecasting weather patterns, predicting the spread of wildfires, or modeling sea-level changes, machine learning has proven to be an indispensable tool.

3.6. Cybersecurity in Climate Research

The reliance on digital technologies and the internet for data collection, storage, and analysis also brings about new challenges, particularly in terms of data security. Given the sensitive nature of climate data and the potential impacts of its misuse, cybersecurity has become an imperative in climate research.

Implementing measures such as encryption, secure data backups, multi-factor authentication, and intrusion detection systems are crucial to protecting sensitive climate data. Additionally, promoting cybersecurity best practices and building a cyber-aware culture within research organizations is important for comprehensive data protection.

In conclusion, technology's role in climate change research is profound and multifaceted. From data collection to advanced analytics, technological breakthroughs have led to a more rounded understanding of our changing climate. As technology continues to evolve, there's no doubt it will open up new avenues for climate change research and continue playing a vital role in shaping the strategies for a sustainable future.

Chapter 4. Understanding the Cyber Threat Landscape

To comprehend the full scope of environmental cybersecurity, it is necessary to dive deep into the vast and intricate domain of cyber threats. This understanding is crucial to constructing robust safeguards for the confidential and sensitive information integral to climate change research. Here, we focus on elucidating the complex universe of cyber threats relevant to eco-data protection and climate change systems.

4.1. The Nature of Cyber Threats

Cyber threats are a pervasive issue in today's digital-focused world, reaching every corner of our society. In the context of climate change research, these threats can take numerous forms, each with its own characteristics and implications.

A **cyber attack** is a deliberate exploitation of computer systems or networks, launched by individuals or organizations with malicious intent. They range from data breaches to system disturbances often with devastating consequences. For climate change research, these could manifest as sabotage of data collection efforts, manipulation of crucial statistics, or unauthorized access to confidential research.

Underlying every cyber attack is a **vulnerability**, a flaw or weakness that can be exploited, either in a system's design, implementation, operation, or internal control. In the sphere of environmental science, these vulnerabilities might exist in remotely operated sensing equipment, data transmission protocols, or even within the data repositories themselves.

Conversely, a **cyber threat** is the potential of a malicious attempt to damage or disrupt a computer network or system. It symbolizes the risks and potential damage associated with cyber-attacks and the vulnerabilities they exploit. Understanding these threats, their sources, and their potential impacts are an essential first step towards implementing effective cybersecurity measures.

4.2. Thrust Areas: Common Targets of Cyber Threats

In the environmental sector, some common areas are more vulnerable to cyber threats.

Data Collection: Environmental data is the cornerstone of climate change research. Increasingly, this data is collected using automated systems such as remote sensing devices and IoT-based sensor networks. These internet-connected devices are a regular target for cyber threats intending to interfere with the data collection process.

Databases: Once collected, environmental data is typically stored in centralized databases, often connected to the internet for ease of access by researchers. These databases, if not sufficiently protected, can be exploited for unauthorized access, data theft, or data manipulation.

Communication Networks: The networks through which this data journeys, either from the data collection devices to the databases or from the databases to end-users, are susceptible to threats such as Man-in-the-Middle (MitM) attacks and Denial of Service (DoS) attacks.

4.3. Cyber Threat Actors: Who is Behind the Threats?

Understanding who's behind these threats provides critical insights into their motive and mode of operation. Broadly speaking, cyber threat actors can be grouped into three categories:

Nation-states or governments: These state-sponsored cyber-attacks are often characterized by high levels of sophistication. For environmental research, this could be driven by geopolitical agendas or strategic national interests.

Cyber criminals: Their motivators are usually financial gain, selling the stolen information in the black market, or ransom demands after deploying malware or ransomware into the systems.

Hacktivists: These individuals or groups use hacking and cyber-attacks as a form of protest, often driven by ideological issues or environmental activism. They might target climate change infrastructure to draw public attention to certain issues or to disrupt research they disagree with.

4.4. Tackling Cyber Threats in the Era of Climate Change

Protecting the integrity and security of climate change research from cyber threats requires a multi-layered, comprehensive approach. This begins with a robust understanding of the cyber threat landscape, extending to vigilance in spotting unusual activity and the cultivation of a culture of cybersecurity amongst all team members.

Foremost, the cybersecurity strategy for environmental research must involve continuous monitoring and auditing of data and systems for intrusions, anomalies, or signs of potential threats.

Second, it's a necessity to ensure up-to-date software, regular housekeeping to identify and manage vulnerabilities, and encrypted data transactions wherever possible.

Lastly, it's all about people. Even the most sophisticated technological defenses can be undermined by human error, so it's vital that those involved in climate change research - be they data collectors, data analysts, or policy-makers - are aware of the potential cyber threats and the significant role they play in defending against them.

The cyber threat landscape is a complex and constantly changing battlefield, wherein protecting the vital components of climate change research is of paramount importance. Getting a grasp on the types, sources, and targets of these threats is the first step towards building effective and resilient cybersecurity strategies. Today, as the world becomes more and more digitized, understanding the cyber threats is no longer a luxury - it's a necessity.

In the next chapter, we will delve deeper into the specific strategies and technologies that can help counter these threats, and the innovative ways in which organizations across the world are rising to this challenge.

Chapter 5. The Pivotal Role of Data Security in Environmental Studies

The information age, with data at its core, has brought about far-reaching transformative change in numerous sectors, and environmental studies are no exception. In environmental research, which includes climate studies, biodiversity conservation, ecology, and related fields, accurate, accessible, and secure data is of paramount importance. The quantity and variety of data involved is vast and includes data sourced from remote sensing devices, embedded sensors, satellites, laboratory experiments, simulation models, and more. Each data point is a piece of the puzzle that helps us understand our planet and its intricate systems better.

5.1. Why Data Security Matters in Environmental Studies

Data security in environmental studies is not only about protecting information from unwanted access or malicious attacks. It is fundamentally an issue of ensuring trust in the data, which is vital for decision-making at multiple levels. Whether it's a local community deciding how to manage its natural resources or an international body drafting climate change policy, the reliance on data is absolute. If the data is compromised, decisions based on it could lead to harmful unintended consequences. Therefore, the integrity of the data must be assured at all stages, from its collection and storage to its analysis and application.

In addition, protecting privacy is another aspect of data security that cannot be overlooked. Some environmental studies necessitate the collection of data that can be attributed to individual people or organizations, like details about energy consumption or waste generation. The sensitivity of such data requires secure handling to prevent misuse and maintain compliance with privacy laws.

5.2. The Cyber Threat Landscape

The cybersecurity threats to environmental data are similar to those experienced by other sectors and include data breaches, data loss, data corruption, and data theft. Cyber-criminals can target databases for various reasons: to steal information for financial gain, to create disruption, or act out political motivations. Some might wish to manipulate data to discredit scientific evidence of environmental issues like climate change.

The tools they use to carry out these attacks are becoming increasingly sophisticated. They range from common techniques like phishing and ransomware to more advanced persistent threats, which remain in the system unnoticed for extended periods, causing ongoing data breaches.

Given the global nature of climate-related challenges, data collected and used for environmental studies is often transferred across borders or shared among international teams. This scenario makes the data even more vulnerable to breaches as it may pass through regions with differing levels of cybersecurity protections.

5.3. Strategy for Data Security in Environmental Studies

Addressing these issues requires a synergistic strategy integrating technological, operational, and policy interventions. Some key areas of focus should include:

- Secure Data Collection: Secure ways to capture and transmit data from field devices to databases should be implemented.

Encryption is one of the common technique to safeguard data during these transactions.

- Robust Database Security: Databases should be protected with multiple layers of security, including firewalls, intrusion detection systems, and secure access protocols such as multifactor authentication.

- Regular Auditing and Monitoring: Regular system audits can help identify weak points that could be exploited by attackers, while continuous monitoring can allow the rapid detection of breaches before substantial damage is done.

- Disaster Recovery Planning: having backup systems and a clear recovery process in place is essential to restore operations quickly in case of data loss or corruption.

- Training and Awareness: All users handling environmental data should be given training on data security best practices, the risks involved, and the ways to mitigate them.

5.4. The Role of Cybersecurity Policy and Regulation

Regulations around data security and privacy should be enacted and enforced. These should be includes within the overall data governance framework, which should also address other questions about data ownership, sharing, and reuse. Clear guidelines should be provided to those handling sensitive data, and appropriate actions should be taken in case of non-compliance.

5.5. The Way Forward

As the climate change crisis continues to escalate, so does the importance of environmental studies and, in turn, the need to secure the data involved in this research. It's a perpetual process that needs continuous focus, refinement, and investment. Above all, it requires a global, coordinated effort, just like the ones required to combat environmental issues themselves.

In sum, data security is a pivotal – and complex – part of environmental studies. It is the silent enabling factor that allows researchers to trust the data they work with and the public to trust the findings that those researchers publish. By safeguarding data security, we are not just protecting information; rather, we are securing a fundamental component of our collective efforts to solve our planet's most pressing environmental problems.

Chapter 6. Exploring Challenges in Climate Data Protection

As we delve deeper into climate data protection, it becomes clear that securing these valuable data sets isn't as easy as most people think. The challenges in this unique landscape are multifaceted, ranging from maintaining data integrity to ensuring proper access protocols. These hurdles are not insurmountable, but require meticulous planning, constant vigilance, and innovative strategies.

6.1. The Threat Landscape of Climate Data

Climate data are typically generated through intricate system models and observational tools that capture vast amounts of data daily. This wealth of information is a goldmine for scientists understanding the Earth's climate patterns, but it's also an attractive target for adversaries seeking to exploit, manipulate, or steal the data.

Cybercriminals have become more sophisticated in the digital age, using advanced tools and techniques to breach security systems. These threats can originate from state-sponsored attackers interested in gathering vital information, competitors seeking an advantage, and malicious actors attempting to sabotage efforts or cause chaos.

6.2. Imperfection and Inadequacy of Existing Cybersecurity Measures

Traditional cybersecurity practices are often insufficient to combat the complex and evolving threats confronting climate data. Many existing security protocols focus on static threats and on protecting traditional IT infrastructure, whereas climate data security requires a more dynamic approach considering the rapid evolution of threats. These limitations make traditional security measures potentially inadequate to safeguard climate data against advanced attacks.

6.3. Risks Of Distributed Data Sources

Climate research heavily relies on the gathering and connecting of data from various sources, often remotely located and beyond physical control of the researchers. This presents numerous challenges such as the need for secure transmission protocols, encryption, and secure storage. Each additional data source increases the network's complexity and expands the potential points of attack, thus heightening the overall security risk.

6.4. Balancing Accuracy and Usability with Data Privacy

Climate change researchers deal almost exclusively with non-sensitive "open" data that do not involve proprietary information or personally identifiable information (PII). However, ensuring data privacy remains a challenge. Sometimes, seemingly innocuous climate data can be used, in combination with other information, to draw conclusions about individuals, organizations, or even national security.

While data anonymization can provide a layer of protection, it also risks degrading the quality and usability of the data. Balancing data privacy with the need for data accuracy is an ongoing issue that lacks easy solutions.

6.5. Mitigating Threats Posed by Insider Attacks

While much of the attention on cybersecurity focuses on combating external attacks, the threat posed by insiders – people within the organization who have access to critical data – cannot be overlooked. Insiders can manifest as disgruntled employees, negligent staff, or even moles planted by adversaries. Addressing this challenge requires investment in areas such as staff training, access control, and a culture of security consciousness.

6.6. Maintaining Data Integrity for Long-Term Climate Study

Climate change research is inherently longitudinal, dealing with data sets that span years or often decades. Maintaining the integrity of this long-term data raises significant challenges. As the environment and technology advances, ensuring data comparability while projecting future trends becomes a complex task. Further, securing archival data poses unique hurdles because breaches could alter historical records, thereby distorting research findings.

Operating around these potential pitfalls, climate data security becomes a task of immense responsibility. Our efforts and strategy against these challenges need to be steadfast, as the stakes are huge – data integrity and security directly impact the viability and accuracy of climate change research which underpins key environment-related policy making worldwide. As we will explore in the following chapters, designing robust solutions to these challenges is not only necessary but achievable with the integration of new technologies and ethical practices.

Chapter 7. Effective Strategies for Safeguarding Climate Research Systems

As climate change establishes itself as one of the most pressing issues of our time, the systems facilitating research into this phenomenon become increasingly critical. Such systems are targeted by a multitude of threats, necessitating robust defensive strategies. This section explores the array of effective strategies that can be implemented to ensure the security of climate research systems.

7.1. Recognizing the High Stakes

Value estimations of climate research systems need to comprise more than just the worth of equipment or data in isolation. The sensitive information these systems reveal have significant geopolitical implications, making them targets for cyberattacks intended to manipulate their outcome or stall their progress. By fully acknowledging this, cybersecurity measures can match the gravity of the situation.

7.2. Implementing Robust Security Policies

The deployment of intensive cybersecurity policies is pivotal to safeguard climate research systems. Policy enforcement should include regular audits, rigorous access control, and continuous team education about potential threats.

> Mandatory access control policy should be implemented, emphasizing the principle of least privilege. Each individual in the system would only be granted the minimal access needed to complete their tasks, reducing unnecessary exposure of sensitive information.

7.3. Upgrading System Architecture and Infrastructure

An upgrade in the system architecture implies introducing segmentation, isolation, and redundancy into system design. Segmentation practices, including micro-segmentation, could be used to divide the system into smaller, isolated units, making its infiltration significantly more challenging.

Network Segmentation and Isolation

> The segmentation and isolation restrict the lateral movement of potential threats inside the network and limit large-scale damage.

Moreover, the implementation of rigorous data backup and recovery policies ensures system resilience in case of any attacks or data corruption incidents. It is essential to routinely review these policies to accommodate any changes.

7.4. Embracing Emerging Technologies

Embracing emerging tech such as AI and machine learning could drastically improve identification and mitigation of cyber threats. These tools could provide predictive analyses, enabling proactive defenses rather than reactive ones. Anomaly detection, one such technique, works by establishing a 'normal' baseline and alerts the system when deviations occur, pointing to possible cyber threats.

AI and Machine Learning in Cybersecurity

The inclusion of AI and machine learning algorithms allows threat detection to be faster and more accurate ⸺ allowing us to counteract potential threats proactively rather than reacting after an attack has occurred.

7.5. Cultivating a Culture of Cybersecurity

A strong culture of cybersecurity encourages all members to actively participate in maintaining and improving security measures. Regular training and raising awareness about the importance of cybersecurity and policy adherence can play a pivotal role.

Security Culture

Promoting an understanding of how individual actions can influence the total security of the system can lead to more secure behaviours and bolster overall protection.

7.6. Partnership With Cybersecurity Firms

Given the sophistication of potential cyber threats, partnerships with external cybersecurity firms should be prioritized for their cutting-edge threat intelligence and specialization in threat mitigation.

Cybersecurity Firms Partnership

A partnership with these firms provides continuous monitoring and rapid response to threats ☐ ensuring the system's ongoing protection.

Overall, the safeguarding of climate research systems depends not just on the implementation of up-to-date security measures, but also adapting to technological advancements and fostering a culture that prioritizes system protection. By adopting such proactive measures, it's feasible to maintain system security ensuring that climate research continues unabatedly.

Chapter 8. Case Studies: Cyber Attacks on Environmental Data

Cybersecurity incidents are an increasing concern globally. In the context of environmental data, the implications can be severe. The following cases take a look at real-life incidents in which critical climate research faced cyber attacks. We delve into what happened, how it was resolved, and the lessons learned.

8.1. The 2011 Attack on The U.S. National Oceanic and Atmospheric Administration

This well-coordinated attack targeted the infrastructure of The U.S. National Oceanic and Atmospheric Administration (NOAA), impacting its highly sensitive environmental satellite data. Covertly, attackers injected malicious software that disrupted satellite feeds important for predicting severe weather conditions.

The NOAA had to cut off their systems temporarily to retaliate and excise the malware. This disruption hindered several climate research processes, including those related to severe weather event prediction. Operational resilience was commendable, leading to a system's revival without grave dissemination of misinformation. This incident underscored the necessity for robust intrusion detection systems and the importance of rapid incident response capabilities.

8.2. The University of East Anglia's Climatic Research Unit (CRU) Hack

In 2009, the CRU faced a serious breach exposing thousands of emails and documents of climate researchers, fondly referred to as 'ClimateGate.' This attack had both significant intellectual and reputational adverse impacts. The stolen documents were leaked, manipulated, and used to discredit climate change research.

The university dealt with the aftermath by tightening their cybersecurity protocol and by leveraging this incident as an opportunity for openness and collaboration with the public. The incident highlighted how attacks could potentially undermine the credibility of climate science and encouraged the scientific community to be rigorous in their data security measures.

8.3. The Australian Bureau of Meteorology Breach

Australia's Bureau of Meteorology faced a serious system compromise in 2015 impacting operational efficiency, staff communication, and real-time environmental monitoring. The sophisticated breach encrypted data files, causing resource drainage.

It was later revealed that freshwater resources data was specifically targeted in this attack, possibly suggesting geopolitical intentions. After an exhaustive recovery process, cybersecurity measures were upgraded extensively, bringing the attention of various agencies on the need for proactive protections.

8.4. The Restoration and Preservation of Historical Climate Data

In fear of data loss during administration changes in the United States, numerous volunteers, fearing political influences, began to store and replicate valuable environmental data. The nature of this task brought significant cybersecurity concerns, including data integrity, access controls, and encryption.

While not a direct hack, this case offers an interesting perspective on the integrity threats that environmental data can face. To address these threats, a 'DataRefuge' initiative was launched, deploying strong encryption mechanisms and stringent access controls, thereby demonstrating how a robust cybersecurity framework could go a long way in preserving irreplaceable climate records.

8.5. The Amplification of Cyber Threats Amidst COVID-19

The pandemic brought about a surge of cyber threats not sparing environmental research initiatives. In this asynchronous digital environment, the uptick in malicious attacks increased, targeting vulnerabilities in remote operational structures. This situation underlined the need for a comprehensive cybersecurity strategy addressing the vulnerabilities intrinsic to remote operations.

Environmental data is fascinating, both in terms of its significance to humanity and the robust systems designed for its protection. It demands an invincible shield, necessitating state-of-the-art cybersecurity measures. As these case studies elucidate, given the increasing reliance on comprehensive environmental data for making global decisions, protecting it from malicious cyber threats is undeniably paramount.

From these instances, the crucial takeaway is the pressing need to invest in cutting-edge cybersecurity infrastructure and measures. Local, regional, and global entities that are linked into this data network must all play their part in creating a secure cyberspace where climate change and environmental research data can flourish without threat.

Chapter 9. Future-Proofing: Anticipating and Preparing for Evolving Threats

Before we delve into the complexities of future-proofing in the realm of environmental cybersecurity, it essential to frame our understanding within the context of the ever-evolving nature of cyber threats. This is an arena that requires perpetual anticipatory thinking as innovative technologies and advancements can inadvertently pave the way for new vulnerabilities. As climatologists and researchers leverage sophisticated technological tools for climate change study, the integrity of their work hinges on the robustness of cybersecurity measures implemented.

9.1. The Landscape of Current Cyber Threats

Understanding the current landscape of cybersecurity threats provides a crucial foundation for future-proofing strategies. The threats can be divided into four broad categories: Espionage, Sabotage, Fraud, and Activism. In the context of climate change research, espionage and sabotage pose significant risks.

Espionage involves unauthorized individuals or organizations gaining access to classified information, which, in the field of climate research, might include intricate details about data collection methodologies, predictive models, and accumulated data. Sabotage, on the other hand, involves the disruption of climate research studies either through destruction of data or manipulation of critical information. As climate change increasingly becomes a topic of geopolitical significance, the risk from these threats is real and immediate.

9.2. Preparing for Unknown Threat Vectors

Identifying potential threats and planning for them is a centralized part of cybersecurity strategy. However, in addition to known threats, researchers and cybersecurity professionals need to remain vigilant of unknown or emerging threats. These can stem from a variety of sources, such as evolving technologies, altered geopolitical situations, and even changes in the behavior of climate change itself.

For instance, as quantum computing becomes more mainstream, it presents a new threat vector. If leveraged by malicious actors, it has potential to break current encryption practices, leading to possible data breaches. In another scenario, advancements in artificial intelligence (AI) and machine learning (ML) could be exploited to manipulate data or bias algorithms in climate change research.

9.3. Techniques for Future-Proofing

Proactive steps can help fortify the cybersecurity stance and create resilient systems capable of countering future threats. Here are some notable techniques:

1. **Adaptive Cybersecurity Frameworks:** One of the key steps to future-proofing is the adoption of adaptive cybersecurity frameworks, which are designed to evolve with changing cyber landscape. They involve continuous assessment and updating of systems in order to remain vigilant against new threats.

2. **Encryption Upgrades:** With growing threats to data integrity, robust encryption techniques should be the norm. Future developments like quantum-resistant cryptography should be considered as they offer more resilient protection against emerging threats.

3. **Multi-Factor Authentication:** This technique has been around

for a while and yet, its importance cannot be overstressed. A constantly updated multi-factor authentication protocol ensures only authorized entities have access to sensitive data.

4. **AI and ML Guardrails:** With growing reliance on AI and ML, it becomes imperative to set up guardrails that prevent undue bias, manipulation, or misuse of these technologies. These guardrails are expected to become more sophisticated as the technology evolves.

5. **Risk Assessment and Incident Response Planning:** Regular risk assessment keeps organisations abreast of possible vulnerabilities in their system. Moreover, incident response planning ensures swift action in the event of a security breach.

9.4. The Importance of Continuous Education and Training

Human beings are often seen as the weakest link in cybersecurity strategy, therefore, continuous education and training for everyone involved in climate change research is vital. This covers not just cyber hygiene and vigilance over suspicious activities, but also overview of potential tactics employed by threat actors, use of secure platforms for data sharing and collaboration, and understanding digital rights and legislation as they evolve.

9.5. Collaboration and Information Sharing

Cybersecurity is not an isolated endeavor. Solid strategies involve collaboration and information sharing. Open dialogue and collaborative relationships among organizations, cybersecurity professionals, law enforcement, and policymakers can yield more robust, wide-ranging strategies to tackle evolving threats.

9.6. Conclusion

In conclusion, as we accumulate valuable data and knowledge in our fight against climate change, vigilance against cyber threats is more than a technical necessity – it is an ethical and societal obligation. Through anticipation, preparedness, constant education, and collaboration, we can build robust defenses against current and future cybersecurity threats, thus ensuring the integrity of our efforts in combating climate change is preserved for generations to come.

Chapter 10. Global Perspectives on Environmental Cybersecurity

Environmental cybersecurity, with its unique challenges and opportunities, is not limited to a single region. Its implications carry global significance—it affects researchers, policymakers, governments, and citizens across the planet. In this section, you'll explore the global perspective on environmental cybersecurity, focusing on its wide-ranging importance, regional considerations, critical changes in cybersecurity, and the transformative potential of increased collaboration.

10.1. Importance of Environmental Cybersecurity Globally

The recognition of environmental cybersecurity transcends mere national boundaries. While some nations are ahead of the curve, many are gearing up to protect their environmental data and systems from an assortment of cyber threats. The motive behind this global concern is the universal recognition of climate change as one of humanity's most pressing issues.

Environmental data feeds into climate models, helping us predict future scenarios and setting a course to prevent catastrophic outcomes. With climate change having profound implications for every corner of the world, the integrity and security of environmental data become paramount on a global scale. Cyber threats to this data present a unique challenge, as the degradation or corruption of input data can lead to inadequate models and misinformed policies.

10.2. Regional Considerations

The focus on environmental cybersecurity varies across different regions based on their technological advancement, the extent of their climate change studies, and their anticipation of future cyber threats.

Developed nations, with a high degree of technological advancement, have significant digital infrastructure invested in climate research. These nations tend to focus on comprehensive cybersecurity strategies to mitigate the risk of data breaches, espionage, or sabotage.

On the other hand, developing nations, though often less digitally advanced, are nonetheless equally invested in protecting their environmental data. Many of these nations are on the frontline of climate change impacts, and the data they collect on local ecosystems is invaluable on the global stage. Hence, they need robust cybersecurity measures to mitigate risks, especially given their typically limited resources for threat response.

10.3. Critical Changes in Approaches to Cybersecurity

With the proliferation of sophisticated threats, the emphasis has shifted from merely responding to breaches to a more proactive approach. This change involves implementing preventive measures, investing in threat intelligence, and establishing incident response plans.

Furthermore, there is an increasing push towards creating international frameworks for environmental cybersecurity. Many countries are recognizing the need for collective security, spawning a movement towards global cooperation and sharing of threat intelligence.

In addition, governments are reconsidering the benefits of open-source systems, recognizing that transparency can foster global collaboration, increase system robustness, and improve resilience against cyber threats.

10.4. Push for Increased Collaboration

Given the interconnected nature of environmental data and the universal threat of climate change, there is a heightened demand for cooperation in cybersecurity. Governments, researchers, and international agencies are seeking partnerships in areas such as data sharing, collaborative research, threat intelligence, and incident response.

Multilateral forums have started focusing on this issue, with discussions involving the standardization of cyber defense tactics, the development of shared threat databases, and the need for global norms in environmental cybersecurity.

Moreover, the increasing reliance on cloud computing and Artificial Intelligence (AI) for climate modeling and prediction necessitates the creation of collaborative defenses. The complex, distributed nature of these systems demands a similarly intricate defense strategy—one that no single nation can craft alone.

In conclusion, the global perspectives on environmental cybersecurity emphasize its vital role within climate change research's wider context, underscore regional differences in cybersecurity capacities and needs, record a perceptible shift in cybersecurity approaches, and highlight the burgeoning need for global cooperation. This collective action is crucial as the battle against climate change becomes progressively steep and environmental data security gains increasing prominence on the world stage.

Chapter 11. Looking Ahead: The Future of Cybersecurity in Climate Change Research

Environmental cybersecurity is a multi-disciplinary field that's becoming increasingly paramount, not just in the realm of the extensive climate change research being conducted, but also concerning our collective future. The fusion of climate science, data science, and cybersecurity presents previously unencountered challenges but, mired within these challenges, lie opportunities for growth and innovation. However, we must look ahead - meticulously foreseeing, planning, and engineering the infrastructure and solutions fueling the future of cybersecurity in climate change research.

11.1. A Picture of the Future

Understanding the future framework of environmental cybersecurity necessitates an exploration of the foundational tendrils on which this domain depends. These tendrils predominantly vibrate to the frequency of cloud technology, big data, artificial intelligence, and the Internet of Things (IoT).

Transiting towards cloud-based platforms, researchers worldwide will leverage plenty of space for the galactic amounts of data that environmental studies generate. Cloud environments provide dynamic, flexible, and scalable storage solutions, a crucial attribute given that climate change data spans timeframes sometimes counting in millennia. But this colossal shift to the cloud comes with inherent security issues such as data breaches, broken authentication, and account hacking. Therefore, security strategies must incorporate robust cloud-protection protocols.

On the other hand, the terrific scale of environmental data is multifaceted; big data analytics will emerge as a staple for scrutinizing it. But the raw size and complex structure of big data complicate traditional protection methods. In the future, cybersecurity must develop innovative techniques to secure big data's storage, processing, analysis, and transfer.

Machine learning, a subset of artificial intelligence, shows promise in addressing big data's expansive complexity. These algorithms can sift through data mountains, identifying patterns and vulnerabilities that humans might overlook. Notably, AI's utility isn't limited to defensive security; it's a double-edged sword that mischief-makers can wield to breach systems more efficiently.

The IoT, a vast network of connected devices, embellishes researchers' capacity to collect data that's real-time and accurate. However, IoT devices frequently suffer from ponderously weak security, making them profitable targets for attackers. Thus, the future of cybersecurity in climate change research will necessitate potent security measures for IoT devices.

11.2. Fortifying the Cybersecurity Framework

The technology landscape is utterly symbiotic - one element does not exist in insularity. Advancements in one domain inadvertently impact others. Hence, it becomes essential to address this symbiotic environment with an integrated, holistic cybersecurity framework catered to climate change research.

Environmentally directed cybersecurity should solidify its foundation by ensuring baseline security protocols. Encryption, multi-factor authentication, regular patch updates, and secure back-ups are fundamental components. However, these methods are merely the first line of defense and must be supplemented with intricate strategies, including the secure development lifecycle, which interweaves security throughout the life of a project, and zero-trust models that emphasize 'never trust, always verify.'

Cybersecurity is also intertwined with legal lines; therefore, adherence to relevant regulations and standards will become imperatively practical. Attention must be paid to laws such as the General Data Protection Regulation (GDPR) that governs data protection and privacy, the Network and Information Systems (NIS) Directive that provides legal measures to boost the cybersecurity in the EU, and the Cybersecurity Maturity Model Certification (CMMC) which measures a company's capability to protect sensitive data.

11.3. Boosting the Human Factor

While technology circumscribes the ring of environmental cybersecurity, humans tread within it. Consequently, the human factor is a key asset - or potential point of entry for cyberattacks.

The future will stretch this human factor across two poles. On one end are the cybersecurity professionals, ethical hackers, and research staff whose knowledge and actions protect systems. On the other are those whose ignorance, mistakes, or intentions breach cybersecurity walls.

To strengthen the former, continuous education and training programs will be essential. These programs should focus on equipping employees with updated technical knowledge, fostering a keen awareness of potential threats (e.g., phishing), and identifying social engineering tactics.

As for the latter, social awareness campaigns targeted toward potential malicious actors can reduce reckless hacking. Moreover, harsher punitive measures and legislation could deter perpetrators from causing potential harm.

11.4. The Road Not Yet Taken

Peering into the future is akin to venturing onto an untraveled pathway - it's spanned with unexpected twists and turns. However, remaining steadfast, learning from mistakes and anticipating risks are all vital components to navigate this journey of environmental cybersecurity in climate change research successfully. We step into this future aware of the towering threats and the unyielding responsibility. Yet we advance with an optimistic fortitude - embodying technology's transformative potential, fueled by human resilience, to nurture this extraordinary convergence of climate science, data science, and cybersecurity.